KT-407-924

Wolverhampton Libraries

LONDON TSO

information & publishing solutions

Published by TSO (The Stationery Office) and available from:

Online
www.tsoshop.co.uk

Mail,Telephone, Fax & E-mail
TSO
PO Box 29, Norwich, NR3 1GN
Telephone orders/General enquiries: 0870 600 5522
Fax orders: 0870 600 5533
E-mail: customer.services@tso.co.uk
Textphone 0870 240 3701

TSO Shops
16 Arthur Street, Belfast BT1 4GD
028 9023 8451 Fax 028 9023 5401
71 Lothian Road, Edinburgh EH3 9AZ
0870 606 5566 Fax 0870 606 5588

TSO@Blackwell and other Accredited Agents

© Metropolitan Police

ISBN 978-0-11-341320-1

If you have any suggestions for improvements to this guide, or enquiries about tachograph enforcement, please contact the Technical Training Wing at the Driving School email Simon.j.murphy@met.police.uk

Printed in the United Kingdom for TSO.

Contents

INTRODUCTION

In 2006 new tachograph legislation was implemented following the introduction of the digital tachograph vehicle unit. In 2007 a number of changes were made to the rules governing drivers' hours.

This booklet contains basic information on drivers' hours and tachograph legislation and is intended as a quick guide for the enforcement officer. It is not a definitive manual.

Since the introduction of the tachograph in the 1970s there have been a number of changes to the way the legislation is interpreted. These changes, in the main, have been fairly straightforward and have gradually filtered through to the enforcement officer without any problem. However, in 2006/7 more significant changes were made throughout the EU that affected both the methods of recording drivers' hours and some of the hours themselves. This booklet attempts to give you the up-to-date rules and assist you in dealing with the vehicles and drivers you may come across during the course of your duty.

There are two ways to use the guide: you can look at the contents page and go straight to the section you require, or you can start at the beginning and work through the flowchart provided until you reach a decision as to your actions.

If you have any suggestions for improvements to this guide, or enquiries about tachograph enforcement, please contact the Technical Training Wing at the Driving School.

Simon Murphy
Metropolitan Police Service Driving School, Hendon

AETR

The rules concerning drivers' hours and the use of tachographs outlined in this guide relate to regulations implemented within the European Union. There are a number of countries either surrounding (or within the boundaries of) continental Europe that are not part of the EU. Although these countries are not bound by the regulations, some are signatories to an agreement that controls drivers in a similar way.

These rules are known as AETR. Drivers of vehicles from countries that have signed up to AETR must comply with them **throughout the whole journey** if it involves entering EU territory. Countries from outside the EU that are not signatories to AETR must abide by these rules (or current EU rules) when in the EU.

It is important to note that all EU states are signatories to AETR. Therefore, an EU vehicle that travels to or through a country outside the EU that is also a signatory will drive under AETR rules (e.g. a UK vehicle travelling to Turkey and back will run under AETR).

The following countries are signatories to AETR:

Albania
Andorra
Armenia
Azerbaijan
Belarus
Bosnia & Herzegovina
Croatia
Kazakhstan
Liechtenstein
Macedonia
Moldova
Russia
Serbia & Montenegro

Turkey
Turkmenistan
Ukraine
Uzbekistan

The AETR driving limits are essentially the same as the pre-April 2007 EU rules (see appendix). It is expected that these regulations will be aligned to the current EU rules by 2010.

Note: Switzerland operates under EU rules.

EC DRIVERS' HOURS – GOODS/PASSENGER VEHICLE: FLOWCHART

You have stopped a vehicle that you think may need to use a tachograph – ask yourself these questions:

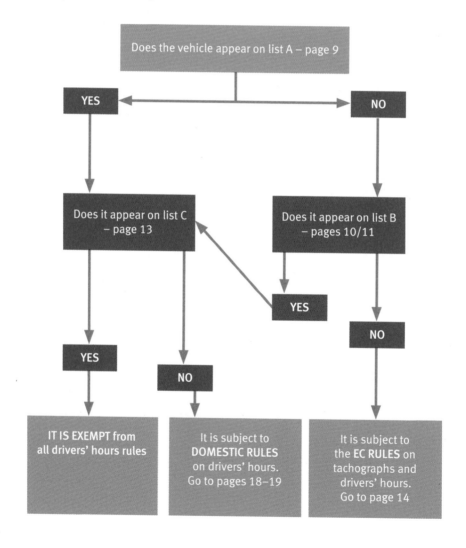

EXEMPTIONS LISTS

LIST A: EXEMPTIONS – INTERNATIONAL TRANSPORT

Throughout the EC, the regulations do not apply to:

1. Vehicles not exceeding 3.5 tonnes maximum authorised mass, including the weight of any trailer drawn.

2. Passenger vehicles constructed or adapted to carry not more than nine persons, including the driver.

3. Vehicles on regular passenger services on routes not exceeding 50 km.

4. Vehicles with a maximum authorised speed not exceeding 40 kmph (25 mph).

5. Vehicles owned or hired without a driver by the armed services, civil defence, fire services and forces responsible for maintaining public order (i.e. police) when the carriage is undertaken as a consequence of the tasks assigned to these services and is under their control.

6. Vehicles, including vehicles in the non-commercial transport of humanitarian aid, used in emergencies or rescue operations.

7. Specialist vehicles used for medical purposes.

8. Specialist breakdown vehicles operating within a 100 km radius of their base.

9. Vehicles undergoing road tests for technical development, repair or maintenance purposes, and new or rebuilt vehicles that have not yet been put into service.

10. Vehicles or combinations of vehicles, with a maximum authorised mass not exceeding 7.5 tonnes, used for the non-commercial carriage of goods.

11. Commercial vehicles that have a historic status according to the legislation of the member state in which they are being driven and are used for the non-commercial carriage of passengers or goods.

LIST B: EXEMPTIONS – NATIONAL TRANSPORT

Vehicles that do not appear on list A may be exempt from EC regulations if their journey does not go outside the UK.

For (UK) national journeys, the regulations do not apply to:

1. Vehicles owned, or hired without a driver, by public authorities to undertake carriage by road that does not compete with private transport undertakings.

2. Vehicles used, or hired without a driver, by agricultural, horticultural, forestry, farming or fishery undertakings for carrying goods as part of their own entrepreneurial activity, within a radius of 100 km from the base of the undertaking.

3. Agricultural or forestry tractors used for agricultural or forestry activities, within a radius of 100 km from the base of the undertaking that owns, hires or leases the vehicle.

4. Vehicles or combinations of vehicles with a maximum permissible mass of 7.5 tonnes that are used:

   - to deliver items as part of a universal postal service

   - for carrying materials, equipment or machinery for the driver's use in the course of his/her work.

   These vehicles shall be used within a 50 km radius from the base of the undertaking, and on condition that driving does not constitute the driver's main activity.

5. Vehicles operating exclusively on islands not exceeding 2,300 km² that are not linked to the rest of the national territory by bridge, ford or tunnel open for use by motor vehicles.

6. Vehicles used for the carriage of goods within a 50 km radius from the base of the undertaking and propelled by means of natural or liquefied gas or electricity, the maximum permissible weight of which, including the weight of a semi-trailer, does not exceed 7.5 tonnes.

7. Vehicles used for driving instruction and examination with a view to obtaining a driving licence or a certificate of professional competence, provided that they are not being used for commercial carriage of goods or passengers.

8. Vehicles used in connection with sewerage, flood protection, water, gas and electricity maintenance services, road maintenance or control, door-to-door household refuse collection and disposal, telegraph and telephone services, radio and television broadcasting, and the detection of television transmitters and receivers.

9. Vehicles with between 10 and 17 seats used exclusively for the non-commercial carriage of passengers.

10. Any specialist vehicle that is being used for transporting circus and funfair equipment.

11. Any mobile project vehicle, the primary purpose of which is use as an educational facility when stationary, and which is specially fitted for that purpose.

12. Any vehicle that is being used for the collection of milk from farms, or for the return to farms of milk containers or milk products intended for animal feed.

13. Any vehicle that is being used to carry animal waste or carcasses that are not intended for human consumption.

14. Any vehicle that is used exclusively on roads inside hub facilities, such as ports, interports and railway terminals.

15. Any vehicle that is being used to carry live animals from a farm to a market, or from a market to a local slaughterhouse, where the distance between the farm and the market, or the market and the slaughterhouse, does not exceed 50 km.

16. Any vehicle that is being used by the RNLI for the purpose of hauling lifeboats.

17. Any vehicle manufactured before 1 January 1947.

18. Any vehicle propelled by steam.

LIST C: EXEMPTIONS – DOMESTIC RULES

Vehicles exempt by lists A and B may be subject to domestic rules. If they appear on the list below they are exempt from domestic rules as well and, therefore, all drivers' rules.

Remember – a vehicle has to be exempt from EC rules (i.e. appear on list A or B) to come within the scope of domestic rules.

1. Drivers of vehicles used by the armed forces, the police and fire brigades.

2. Drivers who always drive off the public highway.

3. Private driving not in connection with any trade or business or with any employment.

DRIVERS' HOURS

EC RULES

Vehicles that are not exempt from the EC tachograph regulations need to be fitted with an approved tachograph (digital recording equipment: vehicles registered on or after 1 May 2006). The driver of the vehicle is required to record the hours worked using the tachograph and comply with the drivers' hours legislation, as listed below

MAXIMUM DAILY DRIVING

9 hours per driving period. This can be extended to 10 hours on two occasions in a week.

MAXIMUM DRIVING BEFORE A BREAK

4.5 hours continuously or aggregated.

BREAKS

Total of 45 minutes at or before the end of 4.5 hours' continuous or aggregate driving. The 45-minute break can be split into two periods, the first being at least 15 minutes long and the second at least 30 minutes long.

DAILY REST

- 11 hours (regular daily rest period)
- 9 hours (reduced daily rest period) – up to three times between weekly rest periods.

Alternatively, a regular daily rest period may be taken as an uninterrupted period of 3 hours, followed by an uninterrupted period of 9 hours

FERRY/TRAIN REST

Where a **regular daily rest period** is taken in part on a ferry or train, the rest period can be interrupted not more than twice. The interruption can be no longer than one hour in total. The driver must have access to a bunk or couchette.

MAXIMUM WEEKLY DRIVING

56 hours (in six daily driving periods, starting after a weekly rest period).

MAXIMUM DRIVING IN TWO WEEKS

90 hours, during any consecutive two weeks.

WEEKLY REST

- 45 hours (regular weekly rest period)
- Less than 45 hours, but no less than 24 hours (reduced weekly rest period). Any reduction must be paid back 'en bloc' to another rest period of at least nine hours before the end of the third following week.

In any fortnight, a driver must take either two regular weekly rest periods or a regular weekly rest period and a reduced weekly rest period.

DOUBLE-MANNED VEHICLES

Nine hours' daily rest within 30 hours of the end of the previous rest period.

The presence of a second driver is optional during the first hour of a double-manned journey. Thereafter the presence of a second driver is mandatory.

GENERAL INFORMATION AND ADVICE

- **A week** always means 00.00 on Monday to 24.00 on Sunday.
- Some countries not in the EC may enter into an agreement that ensures their drivers comply with the rules when within the community. This is commonly known as AETR.
- **Daily rest** must be taken within 24 hours of the end of the last (daily or weekly) rest period.
- There is no **payback** requirement with increased daily driving or reduced daily rest.
- During any **rest period** the driver must be able to freely dispose of their time.

- **Daily and weekly rest** periods taken away from base may be taken in a vehicle as long as it has suitable sleeping facilities for each driver and the vehicle is stationary.
- **Rest** (as opposed to a break) taken in a vehicle can only be taken when the vehicle is stationary.
- A **weekly rest** period must start no later than six 24-hour periods after the end of the previous weekly rest.
- **Weekly rest** can start in one week and go into the next, but it cannot count as rest for both weeks.
- **A break** can be incorporated into a rest period. A daily rest period can be incorporated into a weekly rest period (e.g. a driver drives for 4.5 hours then goes into a daily or weekly rest. A driver finishes a day's duty and goes into a weekly rest).
- The Road Transport Working Time Directive (**RTWTD**) imposes additional constraints on the hours worked by some employees. The police do not enforce this legislation. However, as a result of the RTWTD the EC rules now make a distinction between the 'cross hammers' (other work) and 'packing case' (periods of availability) symbols.

Periods of availability can be considered as a break (but not rest) under certain circumstances. Where the second driver in a double-crewed vehicle is unable to show a break on the tachograph due to vehicle movement, the first 45 minutes of 'other work' can be counted as a break.

Key

- Tachograph charts are printed with a **key** to show the differing thickness of the mode trace.
- Drivers of passenger vehicles on a **regular service** up to 50 km are exempt from EC rules but are subject to domestic rules (page 18).
- The regulations apply to any journey made entirely or in part on **roads open to the public** by a vehicle, whether laden or not, used for the carriage of passengers or goods.
- **Historic status** in the UK applies to vehicles registered for more than (a rolling) 25 years. Each member state can set its own definition of this part of the regulations, so it is possible that some foreign registered vehicles will be subject to a different period.
- Once a break of 45 minutes in total has been taken, the slate is wiped clean and the next 4.5-hour period starts.

DOMESTIC RULES

If a vehicle appears on list A or B and is, therefore, exempt from EC rules, it may be subject to domestic rules.

There are four important points to remember when considering domestic rules:

- If the vehicle appears on list C (page 13), it is exempt from **all** regulations (e.g. the car-derived van used as personal transport: it is under 3.5 tonnes, so exempt from EC rules – list A; it is used for private driving, so exempt from domestic rules – list C).
- There are driving and duty limits for all vehicles subject to the rules.
- If it is a goods vehicle, there may be record-keeping requirements but there are no break or rest requirements.
- If it is a PCV, there are no record-keeping requirements but some break and rest requirements.

DOMESTIC RULES FOR GOODS VEHICLES

- Maximum daily driving: 10 hours
- Maximum daily duty limit: 11 hours.

There are no break or rest requirements for the driving or duty periods, or a combination of both can be continuous or spread over a 24-hour period.

Record keeping

Drivers of goods vehicles that are required to keep records under domestic rules must keep written records in a book supplied by their employer.

Some drivers of goods vehicles that are subject to domestic rules are exempt from record keeping. These are:

- Drivers of goods vehicles under 3.5 tonnes GVW (including any trailer drawn)
- Drivers who, on any working day, do not drive a vehicle to which the driving hours rules apply

- Drivers engaged on domestic work who, on any day, do not drive for more than four hours and who do not travel outside a 50 km radius of the vehicle operating centre
- Drivers of vehicles that are exempt from an operator's licence – unless the vehicle is exempt because it is a crown vehicle.

Light vehicle driving

Where a vehicle does not exceed 3.5 tonnes and is driven in connection with one of the following activities, only the 10-hour daily driving limit applies:

- Doctors, nurses, dentists, midwives or vets
- Any service of inspection, cleaning, maintenance, repair, installation or fitting
- Commercial traveller and carrying only goods for soliciting orders.
- RAC, AA or RSAC
- Cinematography, or radio or television broadcasting.

DOMESTIC RULES FOR PASSENGER VEHICLES

- Maximum daily driving: 10 hours
- Maximum continuous driving: 5.5 hours, after which a break of 30 minutes must be taken.

Alternatively, a 30-minute break after up to 8.5 hours' driving – provided that the period of driving includes breaks amounting to at least 45 minutes.

- Maximum daily spreadover of 16 hours.

This includes work other than driving and off-duty periods during the working day.

- Minimum daily rest of 10 hours, reducible to 8.5 hours on not more than three occasions a week.
- Weekly rest of not less than 24 hours in any two consecutive fixed weeks.

MIXED DRIVING

In certain circumstances a driver may drive both a vehicle covered by EC rules and one that comes under domestic rules – for example, a transport company that owns a 44-tonne articulated lorry that has a tachograph (EC rules apply), and a 3.5-tonne transit van that does not have a tachograph (domestic rules apply). A driver for the company may be asked to drive both types of vehicle during the same week, or even on the same day.

A driver can either stick to EC rules when driving each vehicle, or combine the EC rules with domestic rules. If he/she does, the driver cannot exceed EC drivers' hours limits when driving the EC vehicle, but can drive up to the domestic rules limits in the non-EC vehicle.

This means, for an individual driver, if the articulated lorry was driven for 10 hours, the transit van could not be used that day. If, however, the lorry was driven for nine hours, the van could be driven for a further hour.

If any 'EC rules' (in-scope) driving is done in a week, the driver must observe the EC weekly rest periods for that week and a daily rest period on each day that any in-scope driving is completed.

PRODUCTION REQUIREMENTS

There are rules to control the maximum number of charts a driver is allowed to have with them and the minimum number they are required to produce to an enforcement officer.

EC RULES

The driver should return any charts, record sheets or printouts to the operator within a period of 42 (calendar) days starting after the day to which the document relates.

This is to ensure that the operator gets sight of the driver's charts and can rectify any bad practice.

The driver must produce:

1. All charts for the current day and the previous 28 calendar days

2. A driver card, if they hold one

3. Any manual records or printouts legally required for the periods mentioned in 1 and 2 above.

Manual records can be entered on a tachograph chart (a grid is printed on the rear of most charts) if:

- The VU becomes defective

- The driver is working away from the vehicle

- Extent of rest is highlighted.

Printouts must be obtained from a digital VU under certain circumstances – see the section on digital tachograph instrument/VUs on page 34.

DOMESTIC RULES

The driver must produce a log book if records are applicable. Alternatively, a driver may use a calibrated and sealed tachograph to record domestic hours.

TACHOGRAPH INSTRUMENTS/VU (VEHICLE UNIT)

ANALOGUE

These requirements apply to analogue instruments **only.** A new set of rules have been written for digital (vehicle) units.

TYPES

There are several basic types of analogue tachograph in current use, and two prominent manufacturers: Lucas Keinzle (LK), which became Mannesman Keinzle and then Siemens VDO; and Stoneridge, formerly Veeder Root, which are often fitted to Scania vehicles

LK 1318

(and Veeder Root 8400)

Self-diagnostics

Automatic recording of driving activity – there is no steering wheel symbol above the mode switch for driver one

Two-person operation – when the instrument head is opened, driver one's chart is seen. A plate is lifted to expose driver two's chart. When drivers swap positions, charts must swap positions

LK 1319

(common fitment in pre-2006 Mercedes Sprinter van and Actros LGV)

Self-diagnostics

Automatic recording of driving activity

Two-person operation

Chart eject

22

EGK 100
(some Volvo FH/FM series)

Self-diagnostics

Two-person operation

Automatic recording of
driving activity

Chart release

Driver mode switches

Modular tachographs are designed to fit into ISO radio apertures and are not located in the vehicle's dashboard in front of the driver (unlike conventional analogue units). Their mounting may look similar to digital VUs.

Chart eject   Menu

LK 1324

Self-diagnostics

Automatic recording of driving activity

Two-person operation

Up to 126 errors stored in memory

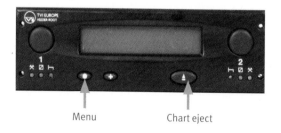

Menu   Chart eject

Stoneridge 2400

Self-diagnostics

Automatic recording of driving activity

Two-person operation

Will not allow chart to be used for over 24 hours

Modular tachographs – important points

- **A significant change with some modular tachographs is the use of only two styli (previously three) to make recordings on the tachograph chart**. This is achieved by using one stylus to record both the mode trace and the distance trace by moving between them.

When the ignition is switched off and both crew members' mode switches are set to rest, the modular tachograph will not record a distance trace, but will leave a gap. If the vehicle has not moved, the trace will recommence from the same point and in the appropriate direction of travel.

- **Manufacturers' plaques** are found in the chart tray.

- **Calibration plaques** are fixed near to the tachograph (including door pillar and base of driver's seat) and must be sealed or tamper-proof.

INSTALLATION AND INSPECTION

Tachographs must be fitted and repaired by fitters or workshops approved by the official authority in each member state.

On inspection (calibration) by an approved workshop, a plaque must be affixed to the vehicle and the instrument specially marked.

Since 1 January 1996, a self-diagnostic tachograph must be fitted and an armoured cable used between the sender unit and the tachograph to prevent interference. In the case of some modular (and all digital) units, the recording equipment is encrypted to the sender unit and does not require an armoured cable.

CALIBRATION, CHECKS AND SEALING

A calibration plaque will show:

- Date of test
- 'l' effective tyre circumference
- 'w' revs/km
- Name and address of calibration centre
- Seal code of centre

- Registration number of vehicle (optional).

A calibration must take place:

- After installation
- Six years after last calibration
- After every disturbance where 'w' (turns/distance ratio) may have been altered
- After every change of tyre circumference 'l' (beyond tolerances).

The tachograph must be checked every two years.

A calibration plaque (giving the date the calibration was carried out) must be fitted in the vehicle – most are fitted in the instrument. There is no requirement to fit a two-year check plaque.

Calibration plaques are usually white and some have a red border. In LK 1318 VUs they are found inside the head, mounted on the side. In 2400 and 1324 (modular) VUs they may be revealed when the chart tray is opened or affixed near to the VU. The 1319s are found near the manufacturer's plate.

DATA PLATES/DESCRIPTIVE PLAQUES

Tachographs must be type approved. The approval number will be displayed on the manufacturer's data plate (silver or black), which is usually fixed to the tachograph. In modular VUs the data plate is found by opening the chart tray.

The plate will display an **e number** followed by a **two- or three-digit number.**

two- or three- digit number

This should match the e number displayed on the rear of the chart used and one other number from the adjoining sequence. If it does not, the chart is not compatible with the tachograph.

For example:

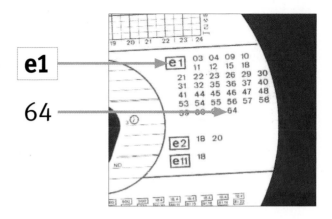

This is the only test of compatibility between the chart and the VU. If the driver produces a number of different charts, each with different maximum speed recording capabilities, the charts are all compatible if the e numbers on the data plate and charts match.

CHARTS

Tachograph charts are easily marked and must be handled with care. An enforcement officer should endorse charts when they are removed from the tachograph for inspection. The officer's divisional/warrant number, unit, and the unit's phone number should be entered, along with the date and time. The endorsement can be made on the front or rear of the chart. Endorsements on the front should be made immediately before the first stylus traces for that day. (This reduces the possibility of the officer's writing and the traces overlapping.)

Centre field entries should start at the beginning of the driver's activity for the day. These are:

- Name
- Start date
- Start location
- Start odometer reading
- Vehicle registration number.

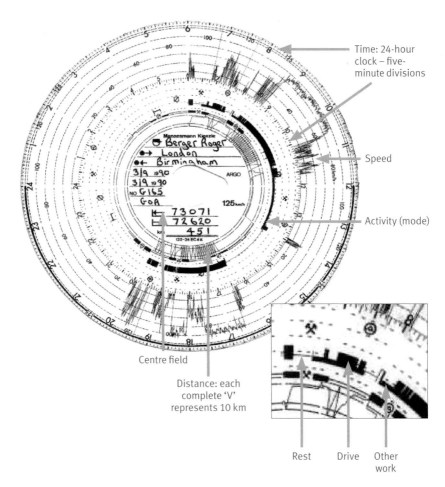

Time: 24-hour clock – five-minute divisions

Speed

Activity (mode)

Centre field

Distance: each complete 'V' represents 10 km

Rest   Drive   Other work

The finishing details are then entered at the end of the driver's activity. There is no requirement for the driver to subtract the km readings.

Remember: a chart without a date or driver's name entered could be completed later to show a different day or driver.

When a tachograph becomes defective, or the driver has been working away from the vehicle and cannot change the mode switch (e.g. from 'work' to 'rest'), he/she must make manual entries on the chart.

These can be written on the front or rear of the chart. However, a printed box has been placed on the rear for this purpose.

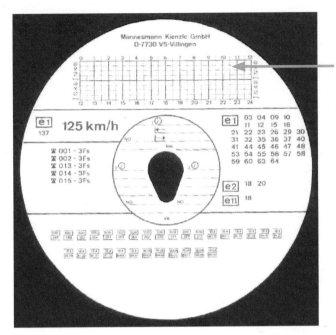

Manual entries can be written on the front or rear of the chart. However, a printed box has been placed on the rear for this purpose.

29

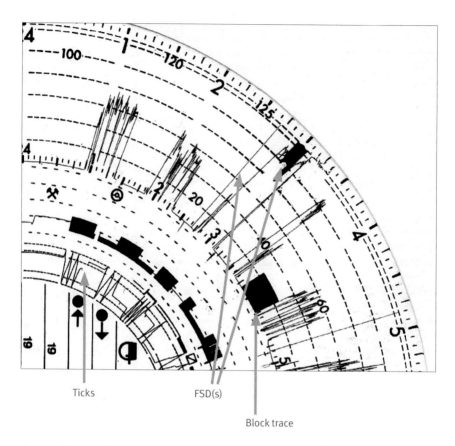

Ticks

FSD(s)

Block trace

Generally, chart removal should not be seen as a fault or an attempt at falsification. The driver may wish to look at the chart to check the hours he/she has worked so far that day. However, look at the chart carefully for any signs that the clock has been altered.

In most cases, an interruption to the permanent power (from the vehicle's battery) will stop the tachograph from working completely as there is no power to drive the clock or the styli – Full Scale Deflections (FSDs) are produced on reconnection. An interruption from the sender unit does not stop the tachograph but prevents accurate recording of traces – therefore a block trace is produced (see above).

Mark	Tacho	Cause	Additional information
Ticks	1318 EGK100	Head opening	Ticks on the chart may appear on all three stylus traces as the head is both opened and closed
	2400		Inserts small mark between distance and activity traces
Full scale deflection (FSD)	1318 EGK100	Constant power (battery) interruption	Continual power interruptions (e.g. connected via a flasher unit) may appear similar to a block trace
FSD	1319 1324	Chart ejection	
FSD x 10 FSD x 8	1324 1319	Constant power (battery) interruption	
0−30km block trace	1318 1319 2400	(Impulse) sender interruption	
0−40km block trace	1324	(Impulse) sender interruption	

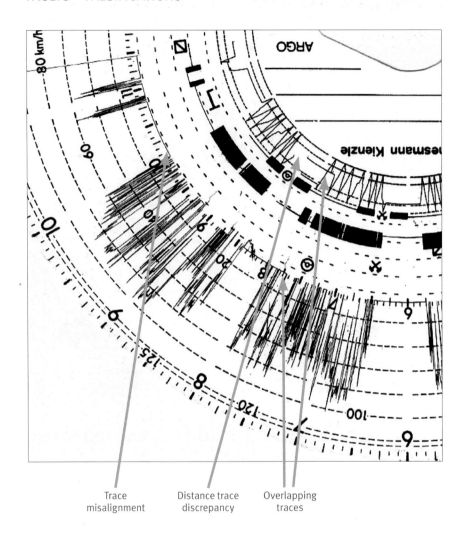

Trace
misalignment

Distance trace
discrepancy

Overlapping
traces

Mark	Tacho	Cause	Additional information
Trace misalignment	1318	Speed stylus bent down	To disguise excessive speed
		Head not properly closed	Usually, distance and mode traces will not be visible
Trace discrepancy	1318 1319	Vehicle driven without a chart in the VU	A (time) gap in the distance trace is due to chart removal. If the ends do not match up, the vehicle has moved without the chart in the VU
			The distance trace records in 10 km 'V's. Therefore missing distance will be a minimum of up to 5 km and then multiples of 10 km
	1324 2400		Distance trace is not recorded if mode switches set to rest
Overlapping traces	1318 1319	Clock wound back or chart in use for more than 24 hours	1324 and 2400 – clock cannot be altered without a programmer (except on some earlier models)

DIGITAL

Digital tachographs were introduced in 2005 and are now compulsory in all vehicles registered on or after 1 May 2006 that come within the scope of the regulations.

TYPES

There are three main types of digital VU in use. However, the vast majority of vehicles are fitted with the VDO Siemens unit. Scania mainly use the Stoneridge instrument.

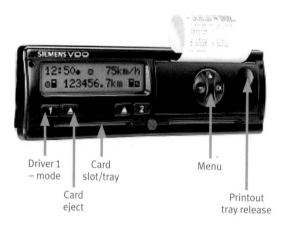

Siemens VDO

Self-diagnostics

Two-person operation

Data storage

Printout facility

Driver 1
– mode

Card
slot/tray

Menu

Card
eject

Printout
tray release

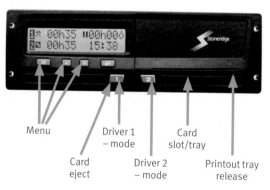

Stoneridge

Self-diagnostics

Two-person operation

Data storage

Printout facility

Menu

Driver 1
– mode

Card
slot/tray

Card
eject

Driver 2
– mode

Printout tray
release

Another company, Actia, has produced a VU with an interface similar to the Stoneridge. The instrument is not anticipated to be widely used, and is not included in this guide.

CARDS

The purpose of the equipment is to store, display, print and output data relating to driver activity. One major difference between digital tachograph VUs and analogue units is that the tachograph instrument itself is capable of recording and storing information.

Digital tachographs use a **card** to access the various functions and set the operating mode of the VU.

Front

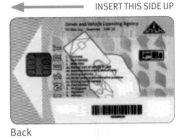

INSERT THIS SIDE UP

Back

There are four types of card:

Driver card	⊙▣	Used in place of record sheet
Workshop card	T▣	Used with a PIN to allow access to the calibration functions. Workshop cards are powerful tools and can only be used outside a tachograph centre for calibration purposes. When not in use they must be stored securely at an approved calibration centre
Company card	⌂▣	Used with a PIN to allow access to protect data contained within the VU and download records
Control card	▢▣	Used by enforcement officers to access data held in the VU

Pictograms

Pictograms are fundamental to any interaction with the instrument. They are used to enter commands into the VU and label information on the VU screen and on printouts.

Printout Features

The first few blocks of information are common to all printouts and include:

- Date and time of printing
- Pictograms showing the type of printout
- Identification of cardholders
- Identification of vehicle.

Subsequent blocks may differ, depending on the purpose of the printout.

```
SIEMENS VDO
A u t o m o t i v e
▼ 29.12.2006 12:26 (UTC)
-------------▼-------------
24h◼▼
-------------○-------------
○ TACHO
  J
○◼UK /DB063121420008 0 0
  08.11.2011
-------------Д-------------
Д VINSIEMENSVDO1111
  UK /BB56CCC
-------------B-------------
B SiemensVDO Automotive
  AG
  1381.1070100007
-------------T-------------
T WORKSHOP 1
T◼UK /WBQOA001420000 0 0
T 15.11.2006
-------------Ⴌ-------------
-------------○-------------
        29.12.2006    1
---------------------------
? 00:00 11:56 11h56
-------------1-------------
Д UK /BB56CCC
          12 km
✶ 11:56 11:57 00h01
○ 11:57
          km;          km
-----------Σ---------------
●▷11:56 UK
          12 km
  ○ 00h00        km
  ✶ 00h01 ◙ 00h00
  ⊢ 00h00 ? 11h56
  ○○ 00h00
-----------!✕◙-----------
✕Д     29.12.2006 11:56
                      h
Д UK /BB56CCC
-----------!✕Д-----------
!○◙   1 29.12.2006 11:47
        ( 2)        00h03
◙---
    -----------------------
!÷    1 29.12.2006 11:44
        ( 1)        00h00
◙---
    -----------------------
!○◙   1 29.12.2006 11:44
        ( 1)        00h01
◙---
    -----------------------
✕Д    0 29.12.2006 11:44
                      h
◙---
    -----------------------
!÷    1 05.12.2006 14:49
        ( 2)        572h5
◙---
    -----------------------

◙◆  .................
◙   .................
○   .................
```

Printouts: general

- **Digital tachographs record and print out ALL times in UTC** (which is the same as **Greenwich Mean Time**). The VU's display can be set to local time.
- It is not always necessary to obtain a **printout** from the VU. Information can be displayed by scrolling on the VU's small screen. An example would be where you simply wish to check the last calibration date.
- **Printouts** cover a period from 00.00 to 24.00
- When interpreting times shown for driving, be aware that the VU always rounds upward to the **nearest minute**. This may have a significant effect on the cumulative or daily driving shown for multi-drop operations.
- Drivers must **print out** at the beginning and end of a driving period if the driver card becomes defective. In such a case, a new card must be applied for within seven calendar days. In these circumstances, the driver can drive without a card for up to 15 days but must keep printout records. This period can be extended if he/she is away from base.
- **Manual records** are entered on the rear of the printout paper where a box, similar to the one seen on the rear of an analogue chart, can be found.
- The language displayed by the VU is controlled by the driver card, but the control card will override this and convert the display wording to English.
- **Printouts** may not photocopy, so it is advisable to obtain at least two copies for any report book.
- **Compatibility** of printout paper to the VU is decided with e numbers in the same way as for analogue units. A manufacturer's plate containing these numbers is displayed in the printout tray.
- It is good practice to take a technical printout and check the set speed is correct.

Printouts: detail

```
▼ 12/12/2004 07:54 (UTC)
```
Date and time document printed

```
----------▼----------
24h ▲▼
```
Type of printout
Driver activities from VU daily printout

```
----------◻----------
◻ SMYTHE
 Albert P
◻▣ B1VIA00234467800
15/04/2006
```
Controller ID
(if control card in VU)
Cardholder surname
Cardholder first name(s)
Card identification
Card expiry date

```
----------◉----------
◉ BUCK
 Andrew
◉▣ CD079856410000 0 0
26/08/2008
```
Driver identification
(if driver card in VU)
Cardholder surname
Cardholder first name(s)
Card identification
Card expiry date

```
----------Å----------
Å XWCV1245891452KNO
UK/QZ50RUB
```
Vehicle identification
VIN
Registering member state and VRN

```
----------Ḃ----------
Ḃ VDO
A123455
```
VU identification
VU manufacturer's name
VU part number

```
----------T----------
T Bloggs Calibrators
GB12546892
T 01/12/2004
```
Last calibration of this VU
Workshop name
Workshop card identification
Date of the calibration

```
---------- □ ----------
B1VIA00234467878


□ 10/12/2004 11:21 ■Ŧ




---------- ⊚ ----------
10/12/2004
602 212km - 602 505km


---------- 1 ----------

⊚■---

  602 202km
 ⊢ 00:00 08:55 08h56 *
 ⊚ 08:56 09:10 00:15


  602 212km  10km




--------------------
 ⊚ Buck
 Andrew
 CD079856410000 0 0
 26/08/2005
 ▲+ UK / QZ50RUB


 08/12/2004  21:25
```

Last control of the driver

Controller's card identification, control date, time and type of control. This space will be blank if driver card has not been previously controlled (or card was downloaded using a card reader attached to a laptop or PC)

Driver activities in a VU per slot

Enquiry date

Vehicle odometer at 00:00 and 24:00

Activities in slot 1 (same format for slot 2) Period where no card inserted in slot 1

Odometer at start of period

Activity, start/end time, duration (* denotes rest of at least one hour)

Odometer at end of 'no card' period, distance travelled since 'no card' period started

Card insertion

Driver's surname

Driver's first name

Driver's card ID

Driver's card expiry date

Registering MS and VRN of previous vehicle used

Date and time of card withdrawal from previous vehicle

```
602 212km        M
```
Odometer at card insertion. M is manual entry flag (entries only stored on the driver card)
Start/end times of activity, duration

```
⊙ 09:11 12:30 03h20

н 12:31 12:59 00h29
⊙ 13:00 14:00 01h01
н 14:01 14:30 00h30
⊙ 14:31 18:56 04h26
н 18:57 20:18 01h22 *
```

н periods of over one hour shown with *

```
⊙ 20:19 21:20 01h07


602 505km    293km
```

Odometer at card withdrawal; distance travelled since insertion

```
--------------------
⊙▮---
 602 505km
н 21:21 23:59 02h39 *
```

Period where no card inserted
Odometer at start of period
Activity, start/end time, duration (* denotes rest of at least one hour)

```
 602 505km   0km
```

Odometer at end of 'no card' period; distance travelled since 'no card' period started

```
----------2----------
```

Activities in slot 2 (same format as slot 1)

```
⊙▮---
 602 201km
```

Period where no card inserted in slot 2
Odometer at start of period

⊢	00.00	08.55	08.56	*
⊠	08:56	12:30	03h20	
⊢	12:31	12:59	00h29	
⊠	13:00	14:00	01h01	
⊢	14:01	14:30	00h30	
⊠	14:31	18:56	04h26	
⊢	18:57	20:18	01h22	*
⊠	20:19	21:20	01h07	
⊢	21.21	23.59	02.39	*

Activity, start/end time, duration
(* denotes rest of at least one hour)

` 602 505km   293km`

Odometer at end of 'no card' period; distance travelled since 'no card' period started

`----------Σ----------`

Daily summary
Activity totals – periods without card in driver slot (same for co-driver slot)

`1⊙⬛---`

Slot 1 no card inserted

`⊙ 00h15   5km`

Total driving duration, distance travelled

`* 00h00   ⊠ 00h00`

Total working and availability duration

`⊢ 11h35`

Total resting duration

`●I⊩ 08:54 UK`

Where daily work period begins/ends

`602 201km`

Odometer

41

2⊙▮---	Slot 2 no card inserted
⊙ 00h00 0km	Total driving duration; distance travelled
⚒ 00h00 ⊠ 09h54	Total working and availability duration
┣ 02h21	Total resting duration
--------------------	**VU daily summary per driver**
⊙ Buck	Driver's surname
Andrew	Driver's first name
CD079856410000 0 0	Driver's card ID
●▸ 09:10 UK	Where daily work period begins
602 212km	Odometer
▸● 21:20 UK	Where daily work period ends
602 505km	Odometer
	Activity totals (per driver, both slots)
⊙ 09h54 288km	Total driving duration; distance travelled
⚒ 00h00 ⊠ 00h00	Total working and availability duration
┣ 1h47	Total resting duration
⊙⊙ 00h00	Total duration of crew activities
---------!×д---------	**Last five events and faults from VU**
!⎍ (06) 11/12/2004 07:43	Event/fault pictogram, purpose, start time
() (0) 00:18	Additional code, number same this day, duration
▮---	No card inserted or card number

Handwritten information

Control place

Controller's signature

From time

To time

Driver's signature

QUICK DATA EXTRACTION GUIDE

I want to:	VDO Siemens	Stoneridge
	⚫ enter/yes ◄ scroll up ► scroll down ⊣ cancel/no	**↵** enter/yes **＜** scroll up **∨** scroll down ✗ cancel/no
1.	**Ignition on** (ensure paper in tray)	**Ignition on** (ensure paper in tray)
Obtain a printout of the driver's activity for today	Driver card inserted slot 1	Driver card inserted slot 1
	Menu button	Menu buttons
Without a control card inserted, the last control is shown with an incomplete control card number	**⚫** printout ■▼ driver 1	**↵** ▼/□ Print ☉ menu ＜ ∨
	⚫ ■▼ driver 1 24h ■▼ day	**↵** 24h ■▼ Print ☉ 24h card ＜ ∨
	⚫ 24h ■▼ day *today's date will be displayed*	**↵** Enter Date **↵** *today's date will be displayed* **↵**
	⚫ *printing commences*	**↵** Select Print ▼ or Display □ *printing commences*

44

2. Obtain a printout of the driver's activity for previous days	Follow procedure shown above until a date is displayed, then: select previous date using ◄ ► and ↵ *printing commences*	Follow procedure shown above until a date is displayed, then: select previous date using ◄ ► and ↵ Select Print ▼ or Display □ ↵ *printing commences*

3. Obtain a printout of the information recorded by the VU for today	**Ignition on** Menu button – press: OK printout ▼ driver 1 ▼ ▼ printout ▲▼ vehicle OK ▲▼ vehicle 24h ▲▼ day OK 24h ▲▼ day *today's date will be displayed* OK *printing commences*	**Ignition on** Menu buttons – press: ↵ ▼/☐ Print ⊙ menu ʌ v ↵ 24h ▼ Print ⊙ 24h card ʌ v v 24h ▲▼ Print ⊙ 24h VU ʌ v ↵ Enter Date today's date will be displayed ↵ ↵ ↵ Select Print ▼ or Display ☐ ↵ *printing commences*

4.
Obtain a printout of the information recorded by the VU for previous days
	Follow procedure shown in 3 above, until a date is displayed, then:
	
	select previous date using
	
	▶ [clock icon]
	
	printing commences
		Follow procedure shown in 3 above until a date is displayed, then:
		
		select previous date using
		
		◀ ▶
		
		and ↵
		
		`Select Print  ▼  □`
		`or Display  ↵`
		
		↵
		
		printing commences

| **5.**
Obtain a printout of events
from a driver's card | Follow procedure shown at 1 above, until:
▪▼ driver 1
24h ▪▼ day

then:

▶
⊗ **!X▪▼ event**
printing commences | Follow procedure shown in 1 above, until:
24h ▪▼ Print ⊙
24h card
◄ ►
▼ ▼

!X▪▼ Print ⊙
event card
◄ ►
↵ ↵

Select Print ▼
or Display □
↵
printing commences |

6.		
Obtain printout of events/overspeed or technical data from VU	Follow procedure shown in 3, until: 24h ▲▼ day	Follow procedure shown in 3 or 5, until:
		24h ☐▼ Print ⊙ ◀ ▶
	then:	24h card
	▶	▼
	!✗▲▼ event	▼
	OK or ▶	▼
	>〉▼ overspeed	▼
	OK or ▶	>〉▼ Print ⊙ ◀ ▶
	T⊖▼ techn. data	overspeeding
	OK	↵
		Select Print ▼ □
	printing commences	or Display
		↵
		printing commences

49

PICTOGRAMS

People

⌂ Company ♟ Controller ⊙ Driver 🕻 Workshop/calibration centre	Relate to those who hold a smart card or to the mode of operation of the tachograph
⊟ Manufacturer	Refers to the tachograph manufacturer – NOT the vehicle manufacturer

Activities

▣ Available ⊙ Driving ʜ Rest ✶ Work	Mode switch symbols currently in use
‖ Break	New separate symbol (only on VU display)
? Unknown	Indicates periods of time that cannot be allocated to an individual driver, due to a driver card not having been inserted

Equipment

1 Driver slot 2 Co-driver slot	Digital tachograph version of the record sheet being in the first or second man position on an analogue tachograph
▣ Card	
⊕ Clock	
⊡ Display	The visual display on the vehicle unit
⊥ External storage	The data is being/has been downloaded to a PC, memory card/ stick or similar

divide Power supply	
▼ Printer/printout	
♫ Sensor	Or motion sensor – the digital tachograph sender unit on the gearbox
◉ Tyre size	
⛟ Vehicle/vehicle unit	

Specific conditions

OUT Out of scope	Allows driver to manually, at the time, show driving time that is out of scope
⚓ Ferry/train crossing	Shows that a driving spell is subject to the rules allowed for embarkation/disembarkation from a vessel in a daily rest period

Miscellaneous

! Events ✕ Faults	The different types of events and faults are described in the Combinations section
⊪ Start of daily work period	
⊩ End of daily work period	
● Location	
M Manual entry of driver activities	
🔒 Security	
⟩ Speed	Be aware of this pictogram – we are used to this being on the centre field of a record sheet for start location etc.
⊙ Time	
Σ Total / Summary	

Qualifiers

24h Daily	
I Weekly	Detail only on VU display
II 2 weeks	Detail only on VU display
✦ From or To	Meaning depends on placing within a combination

Combinations

In theory the combinations of the basic pictograms are (virtually) endless; however, the main combinations you are likely to see are shown below. Whilst the interpretation of some of the combinations is quite straightforward, some are very similar to each other – the order of the individual pictograms will give you the meaning of that particular permutation.

Miscellaneous

☐✦   Control place

✦I⊦   Location start of daily work period

⊦I✦   Location end of daily work period

🕒✦   From time

✦🕒   To time

🚗✦   From vehicle

OUT✦   Out of scope begin

✦OUT   Out of scope end

Cards

⊙▪   Driver card

⌂▪   Company card

☐▪   Control card

T▪   Workshop card

▪---   No card

Driving

⊙⊙	Crew driving
⊙|	Driving time for one week
⊙||	Driving time for two weeks

Printouts

24h▤▼	Driver activities from card daily printout
24h▲▼	Driver activities from VU daily printout
!×▤▼	Events and faults from card printout
!×▲▼	Events and faults from VU printout
T⊙▼	Technical data printout
≫▼	Overspeeding printout

Events

!▤	Insertion of a non valid card
!▤▤	Card conflict
!⊙⊙	Time overlap
!⊙▤	Driving without an appropriate card
!▤⊙	Card insertion while driving
!▤▲	Last card session not correctly closed
≫	Overspeeding
!╪	Power supply interruption
!Π	Motion data error
!▟	Security breach
!⊙	Time adjustment (by workshop)
>▮	Over speeding control

53

Faults

×■1   Card fault (driver slot)

×■2   Card fault (co-driver slot)

×□   Display fault

×Ŧ   Downloading fault

×▼   Printer fault

×Ⅱ   Sensor fault

×Ⱥ   VU internal fault

Manual entries procedure

|►?►| Still same daily work period?

►|?   End of previous work period?

►|●?   Confirm or enter location of end of work period

◉|►?   Enter start time

●|►?   Enter location of start of work period

DOWNLOADING USING DigiDown

Take great care not to have DigiDown connected to the VU and laptop/PC at the same time as damage may occur.

1. Turn the ignition on. Insert your control card into the VU (and the driver card if a card download is required).

2. Insert the SD card into the DigiDown. Ensure that the read/write switch (if fitted) is in the write position.

    Ensure the card is formatted for use. To do this, insert the card into the DigiDown via a USB lead to the laptop/PC.

    Open Windows Explorer and right-click on **Format** on the drop-down menu.

Select **File System** as **FAT**. Left-click on **OK**. A warning message will appear. Left-click on **OK**. After format is complete, use **Safe Disconnect** (in the tool tray) before unplugging DigiDown from the laptop/PC.

3. Locate (and access where necessary) the D-shaped downloading socket on the VU:

   - Stoneridge – remove the printer tray; the socket is to the left-hand side
   - VDO Siemens – the socket cover is located between the ejection buttons. Use a pen to push on the small indentation – the socket cover will open.
   - Actia – the socket cover is located between the visual display screen and the printer, to the right of the OK button. Open by flicking the small 'lip' upwards.

4. Insert the D-shaped plug into the downloading socket.

5. The indicator lights will flash slowly in sequence against each button. This shows the DigiDown is ready for use. If the lights flash very slowly, this could mean you have failed to insert the SD card.

6. Select the type of download you require by pressing the appropriate button on the DigiDown. The adjacent indicator light will flash rapidly. Once the download is complete the indicator light will remain on by this option, but will flash more slowly. Do not select 'all VU' unless you need to – it downloads the speed data, which is the largest data block in the VU and takes a long time. It may only be needed after a collision.

7. Note: if you are downloading more than one option you should unplug the tool and then re-insert it between each download. If you do not do this, the tool may fail to initiate the subsequent download correctly.

8. If the connection is broken (i.e. the plug comes out) the vehicle unit will display a downloading fault which will have to be acknowledged (press OK/Enter twice).

9. To download a driver card, ensure first that the card is inserted, then press the Card button on the DigiDown.

  - The VDO Siemens will show an indicator bar.
  - The Actia alternates between the standard screen and displaying 'Download in Progress'.
  - The Stoneridge shows ↓⏳ Downloading busy.

  The following has been changed on updated DigiDown, where files can be accessed directly on DigiDown using a USB lead.

10. Remove the D-shaped plug from the socket. Remove the SD card from the downloading tool (press it in to release).

11. The SD card should then be inserted into the side of the SD card reader. Note: it will only fully insert one way round (contacts into the card reader, label towards you with the USB connector facing left).

12. The SD card reader can then be plugged into the USB slot on the back of your laptop. Again note that this will only go in one way round (the SD card should be uppermost).

13. Copy the data downloaded to a CD.

CALIBRATION

Digital tachographs are calibrated on installation and then every two years (periodic inspection). Access to the VU for calibration is by a workshop card. Information about the last calibration is displayed on the driver and VU printout.

Digital Tachographs must also be calibrated if:

- UTC is wrong by more that +/– 20 minutes
- There is a change in tyre size (that alters the circumference)
- The VRM is changed.

An installation/inspection plaque, fixed in the vehicle's cab, states the date it passed the workshop periodic inspection.

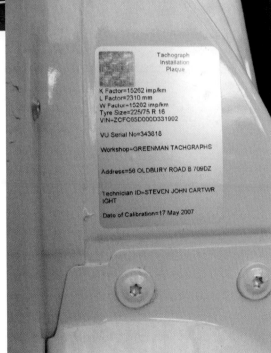

Tachograph
Installation
Plaque

K Factor=15262 imp/km
L Factor=2310 mm
W Factor=15262 imp/km
Tyre Size=225/75 R 16
VIN=ZCFC65D000D331992

VU Serial No=343818

Workshop=GREENMAN TACHGRAPHS

Address=56 OLDBURY ROAD B 709DZ

Technician ID=STEVEN JOHN CARTWRIGHT

Date of Calibration=17 May 2007

APPENDIX

AETR RULES COVERING NATIONAL AND INTERNATIONAL TRANSPORT OPERATIONS

MAXIMUM DAILY DRIVING

Nine hours per driving period – which may be increased to 10 hours for two periods a week.

MAXIMUM DRIVING BEFORE BREAK

4.5 hours in aggregate.

BREAKS

45 minutes after 4.5 hours driving, or other breaks of at least 15 minutes each spread throughout the driving period to equal a minimum of 45 minutes. In calculating when break periods are required, it must be done on the basis that the slate is wiped clean after every 45-minute break.

MINIMUM DAILY REST

11 hours (normally).

REDUCED DAILY REST

Daily rest may be reduced to nine hours on three occasions in a week. The reduced time to be made up by the end of the following week.

SPLIT DAILY REST

Daily rest taken in two or three periods:

- one a minimum of eight hours
- other periods minimum of one hour each
- total rest of 12 hours in 24 hours.

INTERRUPTED DAILY REST (FERRIES AND TRAINS)

Daily rest may be interrupted **only once** provided that:

- part of rest is taken elsewhere and part on board ferry or train

- there is not more than one hour between parts
- the driver has access to a bunk/couchette for **both parts** of the rest
- the total rest period in a day is increased by **two hours**.

MAXIMUM WEEKLY DRIVING

Six driving shifts in a week. The six periods start after a weekly rest.

A driver of a passenger-carrying vehicle on a non-regular service may delay a weekly rest until the end of the twelfth day, or the end of the twelfth driving period. If this is done, the equivalent of two weekly rest periods must be taken.

MAXIMUM DRIVING IN TWO WEEKS

90 hours.

MINIMUM WEEKLY REST

45 hours (normally).

REDUCED WEEKLY REST

Weekly rest may be reduced to:

- 36 hours when vehicle/driver at base
- 24 hours when taken elsewhere
- reduced time to be made up en bloc by the end of the third following week.

DOUBLE-MANNED VEHICLES

When a vehicle is double-manned each driver must have had eight hours of continuous rest in each period of 30 hours. One driver must not be taking his/her rest period while the vehicle is being driven, but he/she may take a break.

RECORD KEEPING

Tachograph records should be kept. The driver is required to produce charts for the current week and the last chart of the previous week in which he/she drove.